Zsa Zsa Tudos

LIFE IS YOURS TO WIN

It all happens in the mind

First Edition

Published by AKIA Publishing

Copyright © *Zsa Zsa Tudos 2020*

Dedication

I dedicate this book to all mankind who possess enough courage and a sense of responsibility to make life better, joyous and more powerful. And to those who have the strength to rise above depression and mental disorders.

Content

Introduction

I am not the first philosopher to observe that the fiercest enemy of mankind is fear. However, not many would take the next step as to figure out the actual origin of this overpowering, omnipresent, life-altering and heart bouncing feeling. Fear is equally in eating or not, walking or not, doing or not, saying or not and having or not. Regardless of the choice one makes, the little devil is always there to doubt the decision. Earthlings have the peculiar idea that making the right decision is vital. However, what they do not comprehend is that every decision one makes is the right one for the given event. The momentary mind-set creates the decision to fit the capabilities of the person. Therefore, every choice one makes is the right one at the time.

Due to the emotions caused by the delicate understanding of happenings, the conscious and the subconscious create filters and gateways through which information comes in and is selected.

However, in the genes earthlings remember. Not only the current one but all the previous lives on Earth and on other planets. There are scientifically proven methods that help in healing and with emotional blockages, such as kinesiology and deep hypnosis, where patients are taken over the bridge, to the past, in an attempt to solve the emotional or physical pain of the present. The success of these methods depends on the reading ability of the practitioner, and upon the patient's openness. It follows the fact that one can only see, whatever one would be able to imagine, therefore, either consciously or subconsciously, understands. This statement might not correspond with the everyday behaviour of the person, for humans put on many layers in order to please others or the imposed requirements of society, workplace and family. In one word, to conquer fear. If a practitioner has problems with seeing past lives on other planets, they will not be able to notice them, and if the patient cannot comprehend the possibility of such life, there is no point in mentioning it.

This understanding is present in the sciences also. A member of this knowledgeable profession learns certain facts about life, past and present, many of them are only assumed or put there for convenience, usually as the starting point. In their work, they apply those criteria regardless, so as to actually narrow the possibilities and the outcome of the discoveries about the past. If you think about it, the past cannot be proven, neither the present, for reality depends on the intelligence and understanding of the person charged with the valuation of certain events. Since the starting point is shaky, due to an ideology, whish or non-proven conclusion, the whole finding will take the turn towards hypothesis rather than real value.

When it comes to mind, there are no general rules to follow. The only fact is given that everything is interrelated. It is the basic and only requirement of the whole universe to exist with Earth and earthlings in it.

The cycle of nature is a piece of clever machinery. Human life is part of this infinite existence that constantly evolves in the interrelations of events. Every living energy has a place in this cycle, humanity included. However, due to the lack of intelligence, earthlings gradually stepped out of it, by imagining that they are above it all, and have the power of ruling, therefore ruining everything. On the other hand, they created God Almighty, who is supposedly in charge of life and death. In this contradictory reality, the responsibility is conveniently shifted over on the shoulders of the Creator, while people of the planet are persistently ruining The Great Work.

This basic contradiction is the root of every confusion, misconception, and misunderstanding in the minds of many.

It is very naïve to think that the mind could be healed by superficial aids such as medication or conventional psychoanalysis. It takes learning, understanding and willpower, to get on the path of joyful living. It is time to realize that nothing valuable comes to you without work, for valuable thoughts, understandings and knowledge are hidden. It takes a committed, curious and life-loving earthling to dig for the treasure without being satisfied by the glittery surface.

This is your handbook to lean on when the burden is heavy. Read it thoroughly and frequently.

Have a nice life!

1.

The metaphysics of Time

"Time is an illusion that imprisoned those without courage"

(AKIA-Path-Finder 1)

The concept is to be at the right place at the right time. The clue here is *time*. Time puts life into a frame, according to which, it should be conducted. Time is the path, upon which one moves. The better one's relation is to time, the more one can achieve. This relation mirrors the state of mind.

In the universe the past, the present and the future happen at the same time. Only deeds carry importance, time is irrelevant. When one needs to act, it is time for it. One must always know when to act, and has to consciously observe it. Deliberately train oneself to wait patiently for the time of acting. When it arrives, it mustn't be missed. That is how time is accounted for in the universe. When I say universe, I mean the ever-expanding space, all the galaxies, and solar systems, Earth included. I also mean every organic energy within the cycle of nature.

However, resulting from the lack of understanding, on Earth people measure passing periods and events by the changes of the physical body. Their whole existence is built around the life expectancy of the suit they are wearing, that enables them to exist on the planet. This habit frames the mind, forces thoughts into certain channels and creates strong foundations for fear, anxiety, depression, and misconception.

It is like looking through a photo album of one's life. Next to every picture, there are details of the place and time the memory was taken. A description is also added, like the first step, the first word, eating alone, sitting up, nursery, school time, graduation, first job, dating, marriage, children, and so on. According to common understanding, these events are the milestones in one's life, and they reflect the unwritten values of one's development in general. In this way, parents are subconsciously validating their actions for future reference.

However, every earthling with healthy bone structure would be able to put one foot in front of the other by instinct, nevertheless not many learn to walk properly. I press the word **learn** here.

Learning is important. One needs to learn to walk, to run, to eat, to speak, to live and all the other so-called natural abilities, in order to avoid physical and mental difficulties later.

A story came to mind that I would like to share with you. Three of my students in their 60s stayed in my modest home for a few days. I cleaned the house, naturally, paying extra attention to the kitchen and bathroom. I put new soap into the freshly cleaned stone holder next to the hand wash basin, wiped off the watermarks from the mirror and the cabinet. By the third day, I noticed that the homemade organic olive soap was reduced to a soft, shapeless substance, lying in excess liquid. There were patches of water in the vicinity of the holder and sprinkle marks on the mirror. I confronted my guests and requested them to demonstrate the way they washed the hands. It was really fun to watch. First, they opened the tap. Then they held the soap in both hands, rubbing constantly while holding it under the strong stream of water. After, without further ado, put it back on the holder with the dripping water. The tap still running, moved the hands under it and started to wash the soap off. Then closing the faucet, one of them shook the water off the hands vigorously, over the sink and reached for the towel. The other two just transferred the hands to the towel together with the dripping water. I do not need to explain the consequences of such behaviour. It is a waste of water and huge disrespect for the soap.

It was time to break traditions. Since they are my students, they took the improved version of handwashing home with them, and haven't looked back ever since.

The story above is a great example of taking certain things for granted. It also shows how much we do not question traditions and hang onto ways we learned in childhood.

The actual duty of the parents is to teach their offspring conscious behaviour and way of thinking. Not of what they know! Or what they consider right.

The problem is that parents are not aware of conscious existing either. They live in the time prison where they battle with requirements connected to certain ages and forced on by society. According to their own status of existence, every little achievement of their offspring would be looked at as the greatest pride or failure. It clearly depends on the mind-set of the parents or actually the leading voice of the family. If the parents are still financially or emotionally dependent on their own parents, and strongly connected to the nest, they would willingly or otherwise, give up the power of decision making over the intelligence of their offspring. Remember, in societies that mistakenly called the most developed, there are many cases when parents are created under the pressure of their own close ancestors. The reasons behind such a requirement are either the validation of their existence towards society at large, or simple boredom set upon them after retirement or just losing interest in life. The other common push is tradition putting weight on people, stating that it is the way of living and the clock is ticking. It is time to produce children.

Bear it in mind that, having children is a choice, not a necessity. It could help the evolution process however, do not do it to pass the time or live up to the time. It could hold you back into the past without realising that you fell off the time machine.

Throughout the ages, on the life path of mankind, times occurred when uncertainty, caused by the forgotten knowledge, engulfed humanity. Fear is a strong and dark matter with an enormous power that, possesses the capability to change the course of history. And these changes are never for the better. Fear brings the dark side out of every one of us and puts life on hold. It takes up a lot of energy and time to hate, be grumpy, sorrowful or plainly sink into depression as the result. These are the times when earthlings brought in or invented superficial powers to ease the mind and living conditions, by shifting responsibility, and devote excess time to the connections. With these exercises, hope was invented and added to the poison of fear. The "*we hope until we die*" is one of the biggest paradoxes of all time. The reality is that with hope living stops. The mind cherishes a favourable outcome of events without substantial work put towards it by the owner. It colours existences, using flattering shades and creates illusions. However, there are parts of the world where hope is considered to be an obstacle to evolve, learn and live. I was travelling on KLM one day, and my eyes were caught on the biscuit wrap. *"Men start living when stop hoping" Arabic saying,* was written there. Kudos to the airline!

Time is a precious vehicle that human beings need to learn how to drive and manage. It is a delicate matter, for earthlings do not really comprehend the important parallel between life and time. It is a continuous and inseparable togetherness throughout existence. You stopping wouldn't halt time, and as time passes, life does too.

According to fear-mirrored information stored, the mind hooks onto certain times in the past and brings them on the surface when it fits necessary. Lamenting about events, either deemed happy or sad, hooks people back to that particular time in the past. Comparison and responsibility shifting takes up the most time in the present, while life fades away, and the future ceases to exist. Let me elaborate on this thought.

The initial approach to life, in general, can be described as the glass half empty or the glass half full. In my writings and teachings, I do not use terms such as positive – negative and optimist – pessimist, because they do not fit the actual mind work I am referring to. Positive and negative are physical polarities and they are neither good nor bad on their own rights. The latter pair describes earthlings who believe, that against all odds, everything is going to come out just fine or no matter how much effort is put into events, the outcome will be painful. These are beliefs of conditioned minds. And like hope, belief is an illusion. It validates failures and achievements in the times of the subsequent present. That is why a therapist's session starts with digging into the past. However, uncovering the time-hooks will not solve present attitudes, depression, anxiety or stress. It is the mind that goes back for help, for it is unable to see or solve situations on the table. The solution is learning. By opening the mind new thoughts flood in, bringing a fresh approach and new understanding. It usually occurs by analysing the picture at the end of the time-hook. Remember, 1. Everything is interrelated therefore happens for a reason, 2. Everything is in constant motion, 3. Earthlings display 100% of their capabilities at every given moment. There should be no regrets and no blames.

Every human being has a different approach towards time. Some want to push it while others prefer to savour it. Both of them are illusions. With the first choice they are continuously in the future

19

and with the second one, they are always in the past. In life, none of them works. Past events should be learned from and closed, so they would be built into the present as experiences. Without closing the past you are not in the present therefore, the future doesn't exist.

LIFE IS YOURS TO WIN!

2.

The metaphysics of The Past

"Life is a constant cycle of personal truth searching"

(AKIA-Path-Finder 2)

Due to its finished and completed nature, the past is not only tangible but free of the greatest enemy, fear. On the other hand, it triggers the other killing machine, regrets.

The past creates the most painful experiences for earthlings and could have a measurable impact, not only on one's life but due to the interrelations, the immediate family also. According to my experience, as a family-relationship-intimacy coach, earthlings belong to 3 categories concerning the way they handle the past.

In the first one, earthlings would remember the past as misery and hardship. It is not only the way of justifying their importance and uniqueness but also letting others know that through suffering, they achieved and deserved the title of *a good person,* living up to the general understanding of the expression. These earthlings always stay in the past without noticing the present and thinking about the future. Constantly seeking affirmations about the past and their well-doings there, and use them as the purpose of being. They do not live, only exist. However, through their melancholic and painful lives, they always make sure to contaminate the existence of those around them.

The second bunch is earthlings who rewrite events according to their peculiar understanding. The past is clear of mistakes, therefore free of responsibilities. Not even the closest family members can make them accountable for past deeds, words, and thoughts. I remember one of the mini courses I call Q'abble, when through astral travelling I guided my students to face up to ailing past events. Even though, they were all professionals in the spiritual field, they arrived back with anger, almost hatred towards their ancestors, blaming them for every sorrow they went through in the past.

The third group is people who understand that life should be lived awoken. It means that experiences are needed to keep the fire burning and the mind open. Responsibility should be taken for the self, and due to the interrelations of energies, also for the deeds of others. This is the group that understands the importance of breaking away from the past by solving and closing it.

Earthlings at large like to go back to the past; either to remind them and others of certain events that are considered achievements to boost their pride, or happenings labelled loss or disaster, performed by *the enemy.* In both cases, they are seeking attention and some kind of justification for their own words, deeds, and lives.

Unsolved past casts a shadow on future experiences of the earthling. By removing it, the present becomes clearer and ready to provide a strong base for the future. Earthlings are here to evolve into the highest possible state when they become the light itself. This journey – I usually refer to as the Lightworker's path - is only possible by constantly clearing the rubbles of the unfinished events in the past. Regardless of the nature of the episodes, there should always be a closure. I like to remind you that everybody is doing 100% of their capabilities at every given moment. It means that nobody should take the blame for past events. There are serious roleplays in human interactions, blended with social and individual expectations that design an unfathomable world for each one of us.

It is natural that the past takes up the most important period when time is discussed. Regardless of the colours you add to it, either way it still sums up to something accomplished.

While evaluating the past, there are a few rules that need to be followed.

- ❖ Everything is energy and lives in interrelation
- ❖ The 2 poles are in everything
- ❖ Positive and negative are polarities and cannot be substituted for good and bad
- ❖ Truth doesn't exist, for everybody's truth is different

Let us get back to the first statement. When I say energy, I mean it from a physics point of view. There is a measurable constant motion in everything, everybody and everywhere, in the whole universe. This motion holds the energy masses together and triggers interrelations. For a deeper explanation about the energy structure matrix, please refer to my *5 Secrets of the Matrix* book available on Amazon.

The second very important declaration is that there are pros and cons to everything. To fully understand the events of the past, they have to be looked at from both angles. However, the result should always be favourable, for everything is an experience. To be able to value joy, one needs to understand the feeling of sadness. The two opposites only exist together. If you nurture the naïve idea of sliding through life without getting hurt, then you are only floating between planes, and not living. Although it is a fashionable concept, you cannot learn from somebody else's mistakes.

The past only holds lessons, not mistakes. These lessons teach different values to every one of us, depending on the basic knowledge and information they land on. Knowledge is created out of information by experience. Without putting them into practice they are only idle words taking up some precious space in the mind, and since they are not connected to anything important, they create confusion.

Without clearing past confusions and feelings, there is not present. And without the present, the future does not exist.

One might say that there is nothing in the past worth valuating. It was a careful, slowly proceeding and smooth journey. Rules and regulations were followed, and emotions were conquered. Yes, it could very well happen to people. Nevertheless, without the past, there is no learning, and without learning, there is no life. It is only spending the time and circling around in the comfort zone. The past is ideas, deeds, words, and thoughts to build the present on. It is the foundation of Life. However, changing your mind about your attitude towards living is always possible. You can turn around and say, that you are going to embark on a more exciting journey and bravely expand your comfort zone. The speed of this extension is up to you. The bigger it is, the more exciting it will be, and the more time and attention it needs. Do not be afraid of changes!

Regardless of the case, the past should be valued, solved and left behind. I suggest the stocktaking method you find in my *Emotion the machinery of life* book, in great detail.

3.

The metaphysics of The Senses

"Live without bringing shame on yourself"

(AKIA-Path-Finder 3)

We live in a consumerist society where we are led to believe that the eye is the most important of the senses, and we do not have much need for the rest. Through this illusion, the media feeds us with whatever is required to follow their guidelines and brain manipulating system.

As I mentioned earlier, everything is energy in the sense of physics. It means that all objects and subjects in the universe have colour, smell, taste, substance, frequency, and speed. This data together makes up the knowledge of the particular energy mass. They are also either + or − in polarity. The polarities have nothing to do with the airy idea of good or bad. These adjectives only mirror a momentary, and often floating viewpoint of the person involved.

The naturalistic of energies appeal to each one of the 5 senses we possess. There is the sixth one, generally called the third eye, which is the interwoven result of the five. You need to consciously sharpen the five to the point where the eyes can see fragrances, ears can taste music and the nose can feel the touch of a blossoming orange field. It is pretty neat when one arrives there.

The metaphysics of the senses work in close interrelation with the mind. Thoughts and feelings alter the threshold of stimulus and filters are applied.

Eyes are the most overrated, yet the most deceitful sense earthlings have.

With the knowledge fading away and fear settled in, human beings started to rely upon their eyes more and more. As they did, the slogan *I only believe what I see* won permanent residence in the minds of most. The irony in this sentence is that we only observe the light reflected back from the surface of energy masses and not the mass itself. Where there is no light we cannot see. While we are looking at something we focus on one eye. We cannot focus on two, only with one at a time. The choice is not random. The right eye is used when something rational, non-emotional is the target.

The left would go under the surface and find details of the energy. Here is an example: looking at a table with the right eye will bring you the structural basics, such as 4 legs, height, surface parameters. The left eye will look at the colour, material, the shape of the legs and the work invested in the making. The method mirrors the premeditated approach towards the table, whether it is needed mainly for the purposeful structure or as a *pleasure to look at* a piece of furniture. You might consider all angles as important. Then alternate eye focus will work.

Regardless of the procedure, the picture gained will end up in the Conscious and also in the Subconscious, where it is put through the filter of your understanding. The result will add to your experiences in the mind.

The other senses follow suit. Every equipment, machinery and digital systems earthlings use, imitate the human body and the mind. As an example, the stereo speakers and headphones follow the structure of the ears. The two sides catch sounds that are different in quality. The right takes in the lower sounds that are slower energy and the left works with the higher and faster energies. These sounds also go through the filter, created by thoughts, ideas, and misconceptions. And this is the cue here. You hear, you see, you taste, you feel and smell things acceptable by your mind. Babies are open-minded for experiences. They smell, taste and touch everything until grownups put boundaries into their mind by restricting these motions.

4.

The metaphysics of The Family Structure

"You must remake yourself in the eternity of your body"

(AKIA-Path-Finder 4)

A family is a bunch of people held together by expectations, roleplay, and fear.

In the metaphysical sense, a family doesn't need to have blood relations. The DNA connection only applies to the physical body.

In order to explain the metaphysical structure of the family, we need to open the horizon towards the universe.

Everything is interrelated in the whole, ever-expanding universe. The biggest mistake earthlings do that they want to explain planet Earth and humanity as separate entities. This way assumptions are made and stories invented to fill in the gaps. Looking back in history, none of the popular stories stands ground. The universe is like the perfect ashlar in the alchemical concept.

Against all fashionable beliefs, alchemy originates from Egyptian teachings, hence the name Al Khemi. Khem is the name of ancient Egypt and the expression means the Matter of Khem. I do not want to follow this lead further because I would never stop talking about it, and the purpose of this book demands me to get back on track. Therefore, let us leave it as it is for now. Nevertheless, the perfect ashlar still requires some clarification. With this thought, we need to travel back to the beginning of Freemasonry. As it is with all the clear Knowledge, it was totally distorted over time, fell victim to gap-filling stories and explanations, and became the prominent agent for the power struggle of The New World Order. That is why we need the root. Embracing the harmony within the interrelations of energies, in the beginning, these masons were commissioned to build important sanctuaries and centres, manipulating the energies of nature by their knowledge of The Matrix. Their symbol was the perfect ashlar, the stone wall, constructed from uneven and rough-surfaced rocks, fit in such a fashion that was able to provide a strong base for enormous buildings and withstand time. The most peculiar nature of the perfect ashlar is that the rocks are placed together without filling or added glue material. This way the organic energy flow within the construction is harmonious hence follows the matrix of the universe. This is what metaphysics is all about; putting genuine structures together and discarding the non-related speculations. Al Khemi is the teaching of metaphysics, the interrelations of energies.

It shouldn't be a big shock that earthlings arrived at the planet from the universe. The lack of a valid link between the DNA structure of the animal kingdom and humans serves as an explanation. This is an important factor we need to embrace.

There are basically two types of earthlings in existence: souls and robots. Neither of them is better than the other one, only different. The metamorphosis lies in the structure of the mind. Souls remember. In their Subconscious, they carry the Knowledge from the universe, while robots embrace earthly experiences through the Conscious.

More about the metaphysical structure of the mind later in this book.

The family is life's biggest playground, where members continue or start learning the interrelations of events. It is the place for not only mental but also emotional development: the beginning of the journey towards emotional intelligence.

I do not want to go far back in history, why and when the family concept was created because it is irrelevant to our task here. The most important is to establish that the smallest nucleus in human society serves as an imaginary shield against the biggest enemy of mankind: fear. It also serves as an easily manipulated unit in a capitalist society.

As I have mentioned earlier, fear comes from a lack of knowledge. They fear the dark because they cannot see what is there, and do not have the working ability to use other senses. The fear of water comes from not being able to swim well enough to conquer its power. The fear in an abusing relationship mirrors the incapacity of leaving the environment. These are examples of the lack of trust in the Self that is a major issue in the matrix of the family structure. The primary duty of the parents is to plant the understanding of responsibility into the minds of their children and cultivate their confidence and capabilities to conquer life's challenges. If a grownup person – I would say around 21 years of age in today's civilization – doesn't have a strong enough desire to fly out of the nest and set up existence on their own, life would become more and more diluted and slowly fades away; unless an outside influence opens a gate towards conscious living. It also shows a lack of consistency in parenting skills.

The basic subjects of this floating illusion varied throughout the ages, reflecting the overall feelings of societies and human groups living side by side. Today, these feelings are strongly manipulated by the interwoven media that serves the desires of the power clusters fast closing up on humanity.

In the 21st century, the new god Money is ruling, and the lack of it put a lot of strain on couples, families and earthlings in general. Interestingly enough, people with some money are far more stressed than those not having any. Providing for the self and the dependants on a daily basis is in alignment with nature. However, money is not tangible, therefore having it creates an even stronger fear of losing it. The feeling is valid. Due to its liquid state, it can evaporate any time and without excuse. The struggle for survival is created by political and financial institutions to validate their work and take the most from people in the process.

Many earthlings feel that politics are unimportant when we talk about their mental welfare. They cannot be more mistaken. Everything they do, they eat, they think, they say, they wear and work with, is politics, and support the beliefs of the major political and financial groups. This support means that they give them permission to act on their behalf without continuously demanding an explanation for their moves. Unconsciously they give away control over their existence.

Depending on the level of consciousness and relation with life and fellow earthlings, they might finally realize what happened, and start making noises, usually to themselves at first, and to the family later. The latter is very tricky indeed. Due to the absence of consciousness, there are not many families, where you can openly discuss different political, sexual and ethical views, without losing face and respect, or being subjected to some kind of mockery. These conversations, or the lack of them, put a strong impact on the lives, especially the future of the members concerned.

Where there are two earthlings, one of them is the leader. Even in partnerships. One of them will make the final decision. It is valid for families also. The role is not necessarily taken by the member with the highest level of intelligence but by the strongest. Sometimes traditions set the rules about the structure. There are many families today where the children are ruling. Again, this behaviour shows weak parenting skills.

Although scientific researches cannot prove the continuous DNA chain between animals and humans, the media is hooked on this concept. They are also hanging onto the theory that there was the first human couple, created by some kind of humanlike supernatural power, who started to populate Earth. Interestingly enough, these totally different ideas seem to meet somewhere and produce an amalgamated concept that earthlings originate from Adam's rib while still fit into the evolutionary pattern.

This is the greatest paradox of life and the family foundation. The two ideas can only go hand in hand in an unconscious mind, for both are floating in the air without any tangible substance. I do not want to get into the metaphysics of creation here, for it is not the purpose of this particular book. However, I need to touch upon certain beliefs to help understand the metaphysical concept of the family.

Stating that Adam was the all-power mirror of the almighty concept, paved the axiomatic status that females are inferior to males. The thought is strengthened by the much ruling Christian idea of the Trinity, where all three presences are males. The metaphysical - and the original - concept of the Trinity shows the two poles – depicted as a male and a female - that is in everything, work together, help each other to climb the ladder of evolution by creating the balance of the two poles within, to achieve the highest greatness possible. This quality improvement is symbolised by the child, as the new beginning of a more intelligent life, guided by its parents on the road of experiencing and learning.

The concept of the metaphysical understanding is that every human being is equal but not the same. Regardless of your origin, you have the same opportunities to achieve greatness. The emphasised understanding is that personal achievement is not measured by material wealth.

With this statement, we've arrived at an extremely delicate understanding of earthly living and family values.

The first thought we need to familiarise ourselves with is that parents do not own their children. People have offspring for different reasons however, only one is valid. It is a way to test and put forward existing experiences and gain new ones. It is also a lesson in responsibility and understanding unconditional love. I feel weird to put an adjective in front of love because love is unconditional. However, like everything important, it is hard to follow. Earthlings make excuses and invent expressions, ideas and boxes to fit their capabilities and desire. They usually use the main word as the umbrella. Today we hear about motherly love, fatherly love, friendly love, passionate love and so on but none of them is unconditional, therefore not love. Love is neutral. It means that regardless of what others do, love is theirs. Due to insecurity, fear and lack of emotional intelligence, it is a mighty hard task for earthlings. Nevertheless, the easiest ground for practice is the parents – children's connection.

Earthlings are responsible for their deeds, words, and thoughts. This duty also covers the behaviour they should adopt towards their children.

It is the parents' choice to have additions to the family and it makes their responsibility to look after them until they grow into adulthood. Interestingly in societies where having children might not be much of a choice due to life values or religion, people tempt to look after their offspring and unconditional love is understood more than in places where the option is given.

The second very important thought in the metaphysical structure of the family we need to understand is that children are not the extension of their parents. They might take on some of their habits and way of thinking however, it has more to do with observations or subconscious learning than genetics. In Western societies, many people go through much heartache and physical suffering to produce children they could call their own. In the so-called lesser civilised world it is understood that children are precious and also the fact that they need fathering and mothering guidance and attention, rather than a set of people they are related to by DNA.

I am certain you have observed that children of the same couple and similar upbringing, turn out to be totally different from one another. It is due to the fact that under the DNA skin there are souls with individual heritage and adaptability. Without understanding this concept, lives can totally fall apart within the family structure.

The third is that parents are not servants or slaves to their children. They should have a life to handle and aims to pursue. However, their responsibility is to teach values to their children. It is important to look at each member as an individual human being rather than from the relation's point of view.

Earthly living is a school where human beings are faced with challenges to help evolve. One of them is to live and work in a family structure.

However, on the road to achieving greatness, the members need to help each other in finding the self, first of all. This act requires the basic understanding that everybody is working towards the same aim of self-discovery, and despite the role within the unit, there is no such thing as a perfect human being, for flows and merits are essential parts of human nature. Teaching is done by learning. It is also true the other way around. By understanding and embracing this concept, shame and fear would fade and constructive energy would gain a prominent place in one's life.

5.

The metaphysics of Traditions

"The night is not the end of a bad day but the beginning of a better one"

(AKIA-Path-Finder 5)

Beliefs and routines that are passed on from a generation to the next one, we refer to as traditions. Regardless of the weight on them, traditions roll over into people's life unnoticed and without questioning their values.

Tradition is also one of those words that we interpret very loosely nowadays. We use it when we are not certain of something and also when we are very sure of our truth; when we trust something to happen the way we desire and when there are doubts in our mind. The most common way of using this word is concerning our religious stand.

In Europe, and due to the colonisation in North-America and the Latin world, it is almost none-acceptable not to belong to some sort of religious group as if it was the basic requirement of living.

On the surface, we like to favour Far-Eastern religions, such as Buddhism and Hinduism, spiced with added beliefs of our own. We even take on Wicca, the really badly modernised version of the Art of Witchcraft. However, Christianity is the one that shapes our way of living and way of thinking. Not because we believe in it or should believe in it. Although almost everybody goes through a Christening ceremony at a tender age, it is done as a tradition rather than a conviction. We do not think much about this custom however, it has a karmic effect that actually shapes our way of thinking. Like everything with human beings, this belief system is on the surface. When questioned, members of this particular faith would say they believe in the Bible. They do not really say they believe in the Ten Commandments, although it is the base of Christian faith. They place their beliefs in a Book that was written by numerous scholars through many years and introduced as the words of God and prophet Jesus. It is all very well, for religious beliefs supposed to be private, allowing for individual choices. However, it is more and more common to state the Christian prophet as The Prophet and furthermore as The God and The Creator. As if nothing existed before or beside. This is a dangerous stand that shapes our lives unnoticed.

I am not here now to talk about Christianity but unfortunately, I cannot avoid the subject while addressing beliefs and traditions. I find that it is the core of many misconceptions in life. Surely we can agree upon the fact that the belief in Christian mythology comes from fear, and as such, it is the result of insecurity, lack of knowledge and understanding. In the 21st century c.e. (common era), when we use the phrase *seeing is believing*, we readily give into the unknown where our comfort system is concerned. It is like shifting responsibility and allowing ourselves to blame the system or someone else for the misfortune and unhappiness of life. This belief system is very dangerous indeed. Since we give into unknown powers, we lose the driving seat and with it the responsibility for our deeds and thoughts. As a result, we become lost in life that generates unhappiness and sorrow. On the other hand, we are taught to believe that suffering makes us a better person. In many ways, it is true if it is the result of experiencing something new and we learn from it. Self-inflicted suffering is idle and might provide a prominent place in heaven, as we tempt to believe in its existence, even though it is physically impossible. However, it alters the purpose of life and announces Earth an unhappy place to be. This belief system makes us intolerant and suspicious towards those with different beliefs, for we do not understand them, and we don't make an effort to try.

The insecurity we gain from religious beliefs would lead us to become part of the global mass consciousness when we follow ideas without questioning them. We believe that they are a follower of the truth. Yes, but what is truth? And whose truth is truer?

Truth is an illusion, for it is different for everybody. It is the straight result of the intelligence, experience and belief system of the individual or group of people concerned. Bearing in mind the fact that we do not actually see what is really there. The eye initially absorbs the rays of light reflected from the object or subject and sends an impulse to the Conscious and the Subconscious at the same time, waiting for their agreement to create a picture consider the Truth by the owner.

We also need to touch upon the subject of spirituality. It is again a belief that spirituality comes with religion and embrace. I would like to shed some light on the fundamental difference between the two.

Religion is a set of beliefs and practices often centred upon specific supernatural and moral claims about reality and often codified, while spirituality is a path to reach and become one with the Creator Force, who or whatever it is. In one word, religion talks about what you cannot achieve while spirituality shows you the path to arrive there.

The belief system is changeable by experience, knowledge, openness, and tolerance. I am convinced that creating our own private consciousness would raise the quality of life, and we could look upon Earth as the Heaven.

Other traditions include a celebration of wars and related events, to remind us of the violent past.

The metaphysical understanding doesn't allow repetitive commemoration of historical occurrences, for the past needs to be evaluated, learned from, and closed. Remembering them over and over again keeps us from a clear and bright future. Not to mention, wars always take lives, a fact, no human being should be proud of.

However, a celebration of considered milestone achievements, such as graduation, engagement, marriage, birth, and birthday, or anything that warms the heart, is a good closure on the past and a gate towards the future.

6.

The metaphysics of Relationships

"The outside knowledge is the start of the wisdom within"

(AKIA-Path-Finder 6)

Everything what and who we are, is invested into the most important interrelations of all, human interactions.

In today's lonely world, there are many of us finding consolation in the company of animals. However, it is an unequal position, for conversation is limited and your pet is at your mercy. It is a hideaway from responsibilities and challenges. Loneliness comes from within and having any kind of company is not going to change this fact, only conceals it.

Like everything, human interactions are boxed for convenience. We talk about family relations, friendships, colleagues, work connections, buddies, and romantic interests and so on. There seems to be some kind of protocol that states how and what within each package. When you are rude to your mother, she would remind you that she wasn't your buddy, and when giving advice to the latter, you would get the, *you are not my mother* phrase. Your boss doesn't want to be treated like your colleagues and your romantic relationship demands more than your friends. These settings are the parts of the never-ending and always changing scenes on the stage of life. From the metaphysical point of view, all labels belong to the same game.

Each of these boxes would grow into a comfort zone over time. The initial purpose of joining the groups will fade as the feeling of belonging gets stronger. You would learn to navigate within and between them. Making compromises, the ability to give in, lobbying for recognition and leadership grow into valued weapons in your survival kit. Regardless of the status within a certain group, every member is fighting for acknowledgement. The chosen weapon, mirrors the emotional intelligence of the warrior and the target. These battles are usually taken for emotional attachments. When your mother is silently slaving for you, doing your laundry, cleaning your room, cooking and handling all the chores, she is struggling with her low self-esteem as a human being and aiming for some kind of recognition, she might label as love, from the universe. You will take her approach as a duty or affection. However, nobody, not even the universe respects quiet slaves. This behaviour is against progressive human nature and there is no way it helps either of the two involved. If she makes a lot of noise while performing those acts, then she is definitely in need of praises, and she'd like to see you by her side in the parental power-struggle.

When your father buys you the latest iPhone and pays for your amusements, it is compensation for not taking much interest in your life and he is hiding the fact that he doesn't know how to handle parenthood. This behaviour also counts as bait in family disputes. Occasions arise when they work behind each other's back, asking you to keep their generosity a secret.

The examples provided fit the conduct of most members in all the groups. Self-evaluation is either unknown or painful in today's society, therefore individuals rely upon members closest to them for judgement. However, the mirrors are set by the personal interests of those holding them.

The strength of the bubble is not equally important for all the members. Those with personal strive move to the periphery, looking for an opportunity to break free and pursue the interest close to their heart. The escape needs careful planning, for others faithful to the core, will do virtually anything to keep them back. Warnings, blackmail and painting a bleak picture of the future as an outsider would surface, representing the wishes of those remain. These actions test your commitment, patience, and determination for the individual life you set out to achieve. If you yield, you should stay and work for the bubble, until your summon more strength and clearer thoughts for the next available exit. Or just succumb and stay put.

I see these bubbles as star gateways. Each is designed to fit certain energies and support the chosen lifeform. Within, they provide the illusion of security and sustainable livelihood. Nonetheless, they are bubbles, and outside forces, which are designed to override the strength of the glue that holds the structure together, would be able to weaken or completely destroy them. When it happens, the havoc created by the event will push members and sympathisers into the open, to pursue new interests or to fall victims to headstrong organisation bubbles. It is all for the better. Real experiences, life, and thought-changing events only happen outside the comfort zone, when you are on your own, and you think of yourself only. I know it sounds awfully selfish in the fashionable sense. Nevertheless, it is your life and you need to make it work the way you want. Think about it! If you do not look after yourself, you will never have the capability to look after anybody else and your contribution will not prove useful for the groups to which you happened to belong. You can only be truly appreciated if you love yourself. And since you are a human being, you have flaws and merits. You might become a dictator without appreciating yourself but love the power, and conduct your actions through sustaining the fear you sowed into the minds of members.

The key to the metaphysics of relationships and fulfilling interactions lies in certain understandings.

- ❖ Life is yours to win. It is a learning platform where you gain experiences and invests them into practice.

- ❖ All human beings are equal. Under the skin, and regardless of the intentionally targeted social, financial and political background, we are of the same organic structure, living on Earth with a shared purpose of evolutionary growth.

- ❖ Souls choose their families. Human procreation provides a suit for aspiring souls to come and learn the somewhat limited existence on the planet. Families and circumstances are selected to fit prior plans and evolution structure. The soul doesn't have colours.

- ❖ Since we live in interrelations every soul and its commitment to the planet is important. Responsibility for individual deeds thought and words should be taken and extended to that of other human beings.

- ❖ Roleplays, such as parenting, children, other family members, colleagues and countless more, are there to support the learning procedure. None of us carries the knowledge assigned to them but we learn on the road. We excel in some and not much in others. It is vital to understand this thought.

- ❖ Everybody is doing 100% of their capability at every given moment. According to the circumstances sometimes it is more, other times it is less but never below or over the momentary personal best.

- ❖ Emotions are the machinery of life. Without them, the motion of existence stops.

- ❖ Comfort zones are for existing not for living. Answers to questions cannot be found there.
- ❖ Roles should not replace personal aims. Having a role is not life's achievement only a tool through which new experiences can be taken. Being a child doesn't diminish responsibilities and a parent should not forget individual aims and dreams.

7.

The metaphysics of Sexuality

"Wisdom is the knowledge you can make use of"

(AKIA-Path-Finder 7)

Sexuality is the most important feature of earthly existence. It represents all creations. I am not talking about intercourse and reproduction but about the fascinating, ever-changing and evolving life, the wonder of living. The whole existence of earthlings centred on sexuality. What they eat, wear, say or do, ooze their understanding of this interactive art. Their individual approach to the matter sums them up physically, mentally and emotionally. A good healer can make a health diagnosis from sexual behaviour patterns.

From the very first moment of their earthly living, baby boys would favour female energies and baby girls would like males. It is due to their physical structure. They also differ in dealing with the wonders around. Boys look at the global picture while girls submerge in detail.

I am aware that it is a very delicate question in today's society however, the gender of the new-born is important. Souls are genderless therefore when they arrive at a procreated physical body to start the new life on the planet, they need strong guidance in order to avoid more confusion. It is down to the parents to establish certain understandings to help children. More about this subject in our parenting webinars.

Due to ignorance, there are many misconceptions surrounding this subject.

- ❖ Sexuality is not intercourse. It is one, two or more organic energies engaging in exchange and blending.
- ❖ From the metaphysical point of view, there are no hetero, homo, bi, pan, and asexuality, only sexuality. The how and with whom doesn't make any difference. Manmade rules mirror ignorance and fear.
- ❖ It works with all the five senses.
- ❖ It all happens in the mind. The quality of sexuality depends on the emotional intelligence of the persons involved.
- ❖ Mutual respect is the ground rule.

❖ The two genders are equal, however, totally different. It is not gender bias to establish this fact. They represent the two poles. The excitement derives from the pulling-pushing powers of the two polarities.

❖ Males and females need different approaches due to their brain structure. The sexual centre of a male is next to the seeing centre and a female has it next to the hearing centre. They have to be stimulated accordingly.

❖ One's sex-drive is monitored by the mind. Gender has no saying in it. It means that by mature, females have an equal desire for intimacy as men do. Only their mind is more brainwashed by rules and ideas invented by males, to provide them with the upper hand.

❖ Since it is life itself, dealing with, and learning about sexuality should be the priority of every healthy earthling. None of the bubbles work without satisfying energy exchanges.

❖ Giving it up or running away from it would stop the flow of the elixir of life.

8.

The metaphysics of The Mind

"Material wealth you can inherit, however, true dignity you need to work for"

(AKIA-Path-Finder 8)

The more you understand, the happier you'll be, because it is all in the mind.

As the philosophy, that observes and teaches the interrelation between the unseen soul and the cosmic knowledge, **AKIA** gives you free hands to discover and open the depth of the Universe and the mind.

In everyday living Earthlings go through traumas, mishaps, joy, happiness, pleasure, hatred, envy, devilishness, fear, sadness, pain, love and other controversial emotions, and not many of us understand that all our deeds and feelings actually spring from the mind.

The Mind is a management centre, where the data - that is stored in the filing cabinet, called Brain - is processed.

In the metaphysical understanding, the mind of a soul living on Earth has 4 compartments. Each is assigned to one of the 4 basic elements that we all contain in the physical body. These are as follows:

- ❖ The Conscious – *Earth element*
- ❖ The Subconscious – *Water element*
- ❖ The Ego – *Air element*
- ❖ The Pineal Gland – *Fire element*

As we already established, everything is interrelated. Therefore elaborating on one point will open all the avenues eventually. However, this book has a certain goal, therefore I need to cut the side roads short. If you would like to know more about the effects of the elements, please visit akiaphilosophy.com.

In the case of the mind, **The Pineal Gland** is the starting point, the 0000 as Sheldon would say in the Big Bang Theory. It contains the untouched, perfect structure of the universe, and since everything is interrelated, it is axiomatic that this format is the key to all creations within. Folders in **The Pineal Gland** contain The Akashic Records of planets and souls. These are pure numeric translations of energy substances, untouched by mankind, or anybody else, as the matter of fact. When certain evolutionary states are reached, the data slowly makes its way into **The Subconscious** for further assistance.

It is said by few, that **The Pineal Gland** is The Third Eye. I totally disagree with that. However, as in everything, there is some truth in this belief. The first contains all the Knowledge and the second is constantly sharpened to seek the Knowledge. The Third Eye is the Sixth Sense that is capable of using all the five together. Naturally, it can only happen if the basic understanding of *everything is energy* is set in. Using the five senses, The Third Eye goes beyond the abilities of each one, and sees, hears, tastes, senses, smells all at once. This way a far more accurate picture of the object is drawn.

There are others, who would urge you to cleanse **The Pineal Gland.** Please, stay away from it. It might be the very last extraordinary gift of nature that human beings haven't destroyed yet. It is a storage place, one needs to learn keywords to enter into and respect to use.

The Subconscious stores the data leaked over from **The Pineal Gland**. Unsorted impulses and emotional experiences from this life also land there.

The Conscious is the place where the clarified files live, representing the actual Knowledge of the owner. It is the Wisdom gained through experiences in this lifetime, ready to be added to everyday practice.

The Ego is the filing manager. Teachings, usually coming from the Far-East, pushing you to lose your ego and become nothing, are agents of the New World Order. Without your **Ego**, you do not live. Having said that, its purpose and structure need clarifications.

I would say, **The Ego** is your darker side that challenges you daily where new information or experience is concerned. It is your fear that holds you back. Nevertheless, getting rid of it is not the solution. Take the tests and win them. The clearer the data in your mind, the better it is for the knowledge. For example, in the back of your head, that is **The Subconscious**, you have certain feelings that there is more to living than what you understand. **The Ego** would say, *no no, there is nothing there!* Your right answer would be a *challenge is accepted* and start digging.

The filing system is your business, **The Ego** is your employee. If it gets confused about your position and unclear instructions, it will overwrite you and take the lead. As in every business, it would be a disaster, for one of you has to assume responsibility.

Let us take an everyday event through the process of the mind.

You walk on the street and you see someone smiling at you as you pass him by. Remember, the opposite genders or the viewpoint are only examples. The impulse triggers your mind straight away, and starts generating thoughts that mirror your evolutionary state, your knowledge, and your understanding. **The Conscious** and **The Subconscious** will create images of the person. If you are a comfort zone being, who is content with life within, you might not even notice the subconscious data, for the filing manager will not emphasise it. However, even though we like the comfort zone, most of us allow the purpose of life – experience and learning - shine through from **The Pineal Gland**, into **The Subconscious**, and manifest in dreams, desires, and fantasies. With the creative power of thoughts, desire and reality produce an amalgamated version of the event that, will win the centre stage of the mind. The more you know about life, energies, behaviours and other human beings, the more colourful and accurate the picture becomes. Desires and fantasies are living products of your creating power, therefore you need mental clarity to correctly handle them. Without understanding the borders between the faculties of the mind, confusion sets, **The Matrix** disappears, and the structure collapses. Remember, you need to hang onto **The Matrix**. The interrelations are keys to living. You are in control. Do not believe that thoughts are just coming to your mind from nowhere, and regardless of what you do, four thousands of them are tormenting you forever. These thoughts are the product of loose ends and miscellaneous files that do not fit into any folders, or the filing manager is doing a poor job. Either way, it is your call to put them right.

Thoughts of any kind need to be monitored and sorted. Major clearance twice a year will do a good job of tidying them. Discard those that do not fit. Fantasies should remain within the boundaries of plausible. I am not suggesting that you need to hold yourself back. However, idle dreams take up space and energy therefore, there is no point in keeping them alive.

As you are gaining new experiences on a daily basis, you add new files to the existing ones in your filing cabinet. When connections are cleared, a folder is created to hold them together. Then it is taken into account as part of **The Conscious**, adding to **The Wisdom.**

Examples of these folders are *Work, Dwelling, Property, School,* and *Health.* They manage the everyday existence based upon the experiences filed.

The greatest challenge to the filing system of **The Conscious** is presented by the Media. The vast majority of the powerful people in the media are ignorant about metaphysics, wisdom and knowledge therefore, their contribution would add to the clusters rather than to the useful. However, since you are the boss, you need to recognise it and instruct **The Ego** accordingly.

The folders in **The Subconscious**, such as *Past lives, Present, Future, Soul Siblings, Tasks,* are parts of the essential information, ready to be discovered, and used as the knowledge, the wisdom that helps with endeavours on the path of becoming better human beings, in the sense of unity and wholeness.

There is also one file, has *Miscellaneous* scrabbled on the front, with an indescribable hue of pink. It stores runaway files that, sort of limber undecidedly between **The Conscious** and **The Subconscious**.

As an example, let us look at the first folder titled *Past lives*. It stores the data of one's ancestors as a soul, the soul-number, the basic abilities, the soul-codes, works the soul accomplished, events it passed through, experiences it had, battles it conquered or lost, and most importantly the knowledge that the soul collected during its lives, prior to the one it struggles with or enjoys here, down on this wonderful planet called Earth.

Although it brings more responsibility, learning is the essence of life, one needs to take on the road towards the greatest challenge of all, Happiness.

9

The metaphysics of Thoughts

"Everything you can touch is lent to you for this life. When you leave you cannot take them with you"

(AKIA-Path-Finder 9)

The impulses in the mind are all organic energies carrying data that have been altered by effects and counter effects, helping or hindering the owner. If the management is good the result would tilt towards the helping end.

The, *everything is interrelated* slogan, offers ample space to the endless, to the untouchable and unimaginable quantity of information, and in its explanations, an extremely dangerous way of thinking.

In this aspect the beginning, the end, and the middle are vague, for every end is the beginning of something, and the middle of another happening. We can say the same thing about the other two.

Knowing all that I would like to start with my beginning. Since this beginning was chosen by my mind, it is not at all illegal to oppose it. However, my choice sets boundaries to the train of my ideas, loosens or tightens their living space. The loosening and the tightening, as the choice of the beginning, foremost depend on the momentary state of my mind, on my relation to the subject, and the goal in front of my eyes. The information I have, my knowledge, my scruples, my upbringing, my schooling, my social background, my pledges, and my conscience, also play a decisive role in my deed. They all, and many more little ingredients send certain passwords to the brain to test and try the key into the locks of neatly filed folders, and into those laying around in lazy untidiness. This action happens in support of the strongest impulse, meaning the most urgent and most important task in the mind that is waiting to be solved. If I am lucky, one of the keys would fit into a lock and I would find few refreshing and helping thoughts behind the door.

Regardless of being conscious - formed under pressure - or subconscious - finds its way without invitation - after creation, the thought becomes an organic energy mass. Imagine it, like the cartoons where the drawn figures' thoughts are being written in a little, balloon-like surface with an end pointing towards the person that masterminded it. This particular Earthling would be the starting point of the thought-energy.

In the universe everything is energy and they follow the rule of *likes attract*. It is true for thought forms also. By popping out of the brain, the thought would become alive. Like all other organic energy forms, the thought would start needing something to feed on. The pointed end turns around and searches for nourishment. This search is guided by the energy of the thought, meaning the words written on the balloon. The natural choice would be the person for whom it was intended. In the hope of reaching it on time, the thought starts its feverish search for the addressee. When found, the thought-form will hook onto the similar energy and make itself heard. However, if the energy of that person has a different frequency, the thought turns and goes back to the sender. Telepathy and cursing follow the same structure.

Let me put it into practice! You broke up with your partner and you are not happy about it. It is the time when you forget about unconditional love and in your thoughts, you wish him loneliness and torture for the rest of his life. The thought-form you have created is a low frequency, slow energy. To find a comfortable base with the addressee, he needs to be similarly unhappy and miserable. If it is not the case, the thought will come back and torment you further. This scenario is set in a fairly clear background. However with the cyber debris, SMS-s, emails, phone calls, and the countless thoughts popping out of people's heads all over the place, one needs to be a master energy manipulator to go through the obstacles they create for the thought-form.

It has been said that thoughts don't count. And words or deeds are far more important. The strength of both lies in the power of mental creation.

10

The metaphysics of Understanding

"Only through the Universe you can get to know yourself"

(AKIA-Path-Finder 10)

By learning, you remember your knowledge,
By practice, you turn it into experience,
By teaching it, you remind others of their knowledge.

You can only learn what you already know, is the key to understanding. It means, that you must have some inclination developed towards the subject in **The Subconscious** and also one or two loose files in **The Conscious**. The information will serve as the hook towards the new ones and push you for more. As they come in, the files need to be sorted straight away, to start building **The Matrix**. Leaving new files unattended will bring confusion and a premature break from the activity.

Ignorance is bliss, they say. But partial understanding is very dangerous. Look after your files and information in your mind.

Let us get back to the beginning. As we established, **The Pineal Gland** is the storage place for the Pure Knowledge. The information here is intact and cannot be altered or played with. To access them, certain codes are needed. It is actually protecting you from the shock and overwhelming weight the unprocessed data could produce in your mind, causing break downs, depression and other types of mental disorders.

The entrance to **The Pineal Gland** is through **The Subconscious**. As we established earlier, events send two different impulses to the mind, one to **The Conscious** and the other one to **The Subconscious**. Like thought forms, the impulses also look for similar energies to hook onto. The slightest inclination towards the subject would retain keywords to drag information out of **The Pineal Gland**. Here is an example: it is raining outside and you need to go somewhere. The impulses you receive will mirror your intelligence, way of thinking, and your relation to life. It could also be filtered by momentary ideas and thoughts you nurture. The data sent to **The Conscious** could vary from *oh, I need an umbrella, I really have to buy a car,* or *why didn't I look at the* *weather forecast.* **The Subconscious** would receive triggers for a deeper understanding of *it is good it rains, the fields need it, I wonder where does all this water come from,* or *all the smog is coming back to Earth with the rain.* These questions would drag some information from **The Pineal Gland** for deeper understanding, and also help establish a permanent file in **The Conscious**. When it is done, your commitment begins and consciously start building Knowledge to enhance your life and that of others around you.

During my many years of teaching experience, I've learned that I have the capability to show the water however, I cannot force anybody to drink it, who is without the hook. One, who doesn't have the basic understanding that life ceases without water might just die from the lack of it.

Regardless of your spiritual and emotional intelligence, there will always be questions in **The Subconscious** that lead you towards a deeper understanding of life, yourself and the universe. It is natural, for you are part of this magic. Without knowledge, living is only vegetation.

Having said that, the majority of the earthly population is without the hook. Fear, ignorance, and misconceptions prevent the bridge-building between **The Conscious** and **The Subconscious,** so the Knowledge in **The Pineal Gland** is never opened.

Do appreciate that most of us do have hardship in life however, the clever ones learn from experiences and use the Knowledge on building a better future.

11

The metaphysics of Emotions

"The light embraces you unconditionally and disappears in you if you let it"

(AKIA-Path-Finder 11)

Emotions are the machinery of life. Without them, an earthling stops living and deteriorates into the abyss of passing. However, passing is not as easy as they might think. It takes many years of subdued refusal to go with the flow, to interrelate, and to be part of this magnificent learning procedure they call life. Far easier, and more exciting to take part in it. One just needs to be determined enough to step on the path and create aims to follow.

Like everything, emotions also come from the mind. It is very naïve to think that we catch them from open-air or even better, we are chosen by them; and if we are not careful enough, they torment us for years to come. I am only saying it because, in my family and relationship counselling business, people are talking about *I cannot help it*. You know, when we say, *oh yes, I am in love with him. I cannot help it. He is nasty to me, he beats me up, but love is blind.* Not at all! Love is not blind but we are! The fear, misconceptions, and lack of information reflect in emotions.

We have a certain preconception about everything, related behaviour patterns, all kinds of do-s and do not-s; some of which we learn watching our parents and the grown-ups around. A big portion of the fixed ideas would come from the media such as films, music and magazines, and what we might refer to as education. There is also religion to take into account, and should not forget the soul's inclination towards the knowledge it has access to.

With this foundation life starts and interrelations begin. Everything we do think or say is energy; as they interrelate, they generate emotions.

As you grow and go through experiences in life, the emotions generated by interactions will change. A type of joke you found hilarious last year might not bring a smile to your face this year. You went through events and interactions of your own, and they somewhat changed your ideas on the subject.

The emotional state of an earthling, changes through experience and knowledge. Naturally, it is a choice to either pursue The Knowledge or struggle through life vegetating.

Emotions are the mirrors of the way one looks at the world. Now you might say that there are earthlings who successfully conceal emotions. We describe nations with the words cool as a cucumber and there seems to be an etiquette code according to which we prejudge people.

Think about it! We do not trust one who smiles a lot or laughs, thinking that he is not trustworthy and serious. It has been one of the biggest problems I have encountered, for I always carry a smile on my face. For me, life is a constant creation, and I feel privileged to bear witness.

Without a subtle grasp, the deep reality of life escapes **The Conscious**. I chose an example the whole of humanity can relate to.

None of the animals we keep in our household are pets by nature. They went through a lot of genetic manipulation to meet the needs of many lonely individuals and to make them housebound. It is a multibillion-dollar industry.

First, there was the internet with the social media choices that encouraged people to chat, not to speak. Without deeper interactions emotions suffered, the freedom of thoughts shattered, and depression emerged.

Following the practice of modern medicine, the symptom was treated by introducing genetically manipulated animals to vegetate around earthlings, who do not have the courage or the life elixir to enter into interrelations with others. On top of all, these people have deemed animal lovers and good, solely for supporting the new business. Since freedom and natural life are taken away from these animals, they rely upon human presence 100% that proves difficult for many owners. This event triggered another vast business, animal charities. I am not getting into all the other necessities and costs entail this venture, only reflecting on the mind and emotion manipulation of the media and multi companies. The mind and emotions turned away from real challenges, where two people decide to learn each other and support the aims of one another, hence offering platforms for learning.

As I mentioned earlier emotions generate the fuel, the elixir of life for the machinery of interrelations.

Everything we do comes from our emotions and our emotions come from whatever we do.

This point is very complex. You remember the comfort zone boxes of role plays we talked about earlier? These are the keys. When you start attending a new box, either out of interest or duty, it is all very exciting, for it is new. You size it up in your speed, and following the level of your emotional intelligence, you either learn a new role or use the one you are already accustomed to and feel comfortable with. Naturally, it is always better to learn. The learning ability depends on your willingness, curiosity and life elixir. The less elixir or drive you have, the slower your brain works. Life elixir is not equal to what is commonly called energy. It is the willpower of achieving, growing and knowing.

Every box – such as parental ground, your own house, friends' house, colleagues, classes, workplace, religious gathering, spiritual learning and so on – has different demands towards behaviour pattern, dress code, subjects to talk about, even the answers to certain questions. If you take all the rules on board and implement them into your own life, it will become a big muddle, where fishing for the right attitude will pose problems. However, there are earthlings, who successfully manage to navigate between boxes, always finding the right tone, clothing, and emotional bearing to fit the occasion.

Nevertheless, in the comfort zones, the possibility of emotional exchange is very limited. Therefore growing, learning or finding and developing the Self is almost impossible.

Do not forget, you are the master! They are your emotions and your life. And the master always wins! Open your mind, your life, learn from events and others: allow your emotions to flow. However, you need to maintain control at all times. Not a tight one, only 2%, if you are brave. Losing the driving seat means that you are not going anywhere, so you miss the experience. You have to shine through every cloud and fog.

So when you arrive home from a party announcing that: *it was great! I got stoned and I do not remember anything* would pause a valid question. What was so great about it? Wasn't it a waste of time and effort? It is only an experience if you are able to recollect it and use it.

Life is yours to win!

12

The metaphysics of The Code

"Imagination is the memory of the soul"

(AKIA-Path-Finder 12)

The code is all the permanent or hopefully semi-permanent dogmas, rules, regulations, moral standards, ways of thinking and understanding. It is unique to every person. As life goes by, more experience is gained that either loosens or tightens the existing management system of **The Mind**.

Social media is flooded by articles, books and advertisements from meditation centres, self-claimed healers and coaches who talk about the permanence of codes, something that is unchangeable, carried from the ancestors through seven generations. I do not support the idea. The trodden path of the grandparents is a lively learning ground. However, this view will transfer the lineage's responsibility for their deeds, onto your shoulders, creating quite an upheaval and many obstacles in life. When we look at the constantly moving Universe we realize that this idea is only wishful thinking by those who dislike change and dwell in the past. Or of those who want to implant fear and with that, a total succumb to man-made controlling rules. It is a dangerous idea indeed. The foundation is fragile and totally dismisses the possibility of the Macrocosm by turning Earthlings into narrow-minded robot-like creatures with limited choices about the future. Only few realise that the taking on the codes of the parents, places the weight of humanity on their existence. It is a chain that is traceable back to the beginning. You take on your mother's code while she is already having her mother's. Your grandmother also has her mother's and so on. So actually you are carrying the responsibility, karma and codes of the whole 22,000 odd years of earthly living.

On the other hand, earthly ancestors mean very little to a soul. Many people follow or relive the life of a parent of the same gender believing that there is no choice; that this path has to be taken for it is karmic or simply fate. Well, choices do not come to you by themselves. One needs to have adequate information to be presented with choices. Everybody has them but one needs to find the path to them and learn to embrace the presented possibilities. For many people having choices is a curse. Different aspects need to be looked at, and decisions have to be made. Work with the changes, fear of the unknown would push these people back into the comfort zone.

There are certain cases when one follows the footsteps of a parent without much thought and consideration, and when reality hits it is too late to stop the motion. Looking at parents as role models can make or break the future of a child. There is far more to parenting than staying together and pretending to be a happy family.

There are also physical inclinations such as certain movements and ways of carrying oneself; likes and dislikes for food, drink, events and so on. As likes and dislikes are in the mind I would not take it for a code. My parents divorced when I was 4 years old. I lived with my mother who was constantly blaming my father for every mishap and every pain, and told nasty stories about him, even though she was already remarried and had a new baby from the second marriage. One day, when I was eating sourcrout, which happened to be my very favourite dish, she mentioned that I was a lot like my father because I loved the dish and so did he. I put the spoon down straight away and had not looked at a sour cabbage dish for a couple of years until I had the opportunity to meet my father and understand him a bit better. I realized that he was a good person so it stopped bothering me that I was in any way like him.

Biological inclinations are very tricky indeed. The physical body is the merge of 2 other bodies therefore there is a great possibility to develop inclinations towards certain illnesses, strength or weakness, carried by one of the merging bodies.

These tendencies are dormant until key energy triggers them open. And here we arrive back to the interrelations of energies, for it is the key to everything. Depending on the relationship between **The Conscious** and **The Subconscious**, one carries a certain emotional state which works as a magnet and pulls in similar energies to interfere with the condition of the existing one. This is how inclinations open and blend into the life of the unsuspecting victim. There is also a time when lessons should be learned, such as blaming your mother for something, and life presents you with a similar situation to make you understand.

There is another expression earthling like to use as a shield and a sound excuse for not doing life-related chores, and it is **Fate**. Similarly to the code, it is deemed inheritable and unchangeable. It is neither. Learning and changing are not prohibited.

Every day I meet someone who would state that life is all suffering. Loneliness, physical and mental hardship are the companions. However, nothing to be done. It is fate. Usually, the suffering is to offer redemption for an ancestor who stepped over a few lines and became an outsider of the law. These individuals look upon themselves as The Good Ones. They cannot be further from it. Since we live in interrelations they poison the existence of the rest of the population also. Through their behaviour they force others to accept their viewpoint. If you think about it, it is a selfish act. They do not help anybody, only destroy.

I have been teaching the highest level of Alchemy, classic Witchcraft, Orixa, Voudoun, Tarot, and other nature-related Wisdom, so I am not bashing the existence of outside forces. However, they are part of the whole, just like you are. Also part of **The Knowledge** earthlings should acquire. They are only supernatural if the folder labelled that way. Leave your fear behind and invite them into **The Conscious** to add a fascinating extension to life. You need to be careful though. Find a good master, who doesn't feed you with imaginary non-sense and tells you that one has to be born with the ability to understand and work with these forces. Remember, every earthling carries **The Knowledge** in **The Pineal Gland**. So do you.

13

The metaphysics of Life

"The real knowledge is untouchable and changing"

(AKIA-Path-Finder 13)

If you want your life to progress, you have to expand your relationship with life. It is like a friendship or a love affair. The interaction is important, for it generates emotions, the fuel that enables you, not only to carry on but to improve.

In this book, we talked about different aspects of the Knowledge, the human brain, and the values a soul should chase while living on Earth. Every sentence has a keyword, the one in this is *living.*

Living is an elevated and conscious state of existence.

As we established earlier, the universe is a matrix. It is logical, for otherwise, it would fall apart. It means that a vast web of interrelated existences creates a pretty neat structure of organic energies. When I say organic energy, it means a living substance. I wouldn't connect intelligence to it because it is one of those expressions that carry a different meaning for everybody. For earthlings, it is given that they are the most intelligent on the planet. However, I beg to differ. Vegetation possesses the laurel for being a perfect link between the micro and the macrocosm, and the most conscious part of the earthly cycle. It is naïve to imagine that vegetables cannot think, hold a conversation or feel. Just because they do not wiggle their tails, they know exactly what goes on around them.

If you think about it, everything was a living substance at one point, sprung out of a blend of energies in the cycle of nature. However, earthlings do not appreciate anything with consciousness they cannot fully control. They struggle hard to bring them down to their own level, where higher energies suffocate. This practice is also common amongst their own kind.

In general, coming down to Earth is a choice. Therefore, turning away from earthly life is not an option. Hiding behind dogmas and excuses, spare the self from hurt, disappointment, and sorrow. On the other hand, it is an existence without the wonderful experiences of everyday events. Living in the physical body, yet putting the everyday maintenance chores on the shoulders of fellow earthlings, is an unfair deed. Furthermore, these beings use the most common blackmailing system, the raising of guilt in the uncertain and undecided minds. They might even say what they do is a sacrifice and that it is done for the benefit of others, sometimes even the whole of mankind. Do not be fooled! It is a selfish act, to serve the ego by seemingly becoming egoless.

I am referring to certain religious groups were collecting donations and begging on the street are part of everyday existence to maintain their idle, unproductive lives. It is easy to say that *I do not agree with capitalism, I do not like the money centred society and so on.* If you don't like it, do something about it. Lifestyles and societies do not spring from the ground by themselves. The seed was sown and the land was cultivated. You are part of it, and as a human being, you share the responsibility with others. It strikes me, how easily earthlings are manipulated and how little they think. Not succumbing to consumerism personally but living on someone, who might not have this convenient choice, doesn't make you a better person, only a parasite. It is true for family connections also. These earthlings are stuck to Air element without understanding Water and Earth. It is an unfortunate situation for without comprehending these two, the path to Fire is concealed. The only way is backwards. However, there is a way.

On the other end of the pole, there are those fully committed to consumerism. They only believe in what they see – which is obviously very limited – build their material wealth, indulge the physical body and go through their chosen experiences in life. This group of earthlings is connected to the Earth element. Sometimes they hit Water and very seldom arrive at the level of Air. Fire avoids this group also.

If I had to, I would definitely vote for the latter. They work, they use their minds and they even exercise their physical body and look after it. They also play with emotions, and one day, they might just wake up with the desire to change! To reach the macrocosmic Fire element from Earth through Water and Air, as the major stations of evolution, is a strong possibility. On the other hand, reaching for the macrocosm without understanding the micro is a definite shift of responsibilities.

Every human relationship is based upon the evolutionary state of the self. In the interrelation, individuals should learn from each other through unconditional trust and love. This type of love is helpful and emotionless; the secret of which is to understand the fact that earthlings perform 100% of their abilities at every given time. It is only expectation that belittles the performance.

To sum up the four basic elements and the evolutionary level, I state the following:

❖ EARTH teaches attachments and detachments concerning material. Without understanding both ends, one becomes the slave to money and tangible goods that prevents any kind of evolving. One might reach the six figures in monthly, even daily income, become the wizard of the stock market, would be able to buy material, take the physical body to another level but conscious living would elude these people. The believers of the material world – meaning, what I see is there – are in this category.

❖ WATER opens up emotions, and presents the possibility of understanding and conquering them. Without this kind of knowledge, these people become self-centred and victims of their limited choices. People with strong religious convictions belong here.

❖ AIR is the pathway between the 2 cosms, the Micro and the Macro. It is a floating existence between two planes where the only possible way out is a U-turn. Gurus and Yogis are part of this group.

❖ FIRE comes from the universe. It is Knowledge, Light, and Wisdom. Depending on your state of mind, this element burns or builds. The lack of experience and understanding would result in burns, while Knowledge, based on a solid foundation would prove building.

The latter can only be achieved by following, **The 4th Way**. If you wish to know more about the subject, please check out my book with a similar title. It provides you with explanations and exercises built from scratch level.

The summary above shows you that you cannot run without knowing how to walk. Look at a lifetime: a toddler runs before walking. He does it by instinct. And because it is physically easier for him. Nevertheless, he has to learn to walk in order to run consciously. A teenager runs up on stairs skipping 2-3 because he subconsciously believes that he created the universe. He doesn't pay attention to the bone structure and the proper way of doing it. An elderly person would savour each step on the stairs, consciously or maybe only subconsciously understands that everything needs proper foundation and attention.

It means that you have the choice of skipping however, you have to come back to the missed steps if you want to walk with holding your head high and looking down on your achievements without feeling dizzy.

The 4th Way is the only path to a fulfilled life. Living through and understanding the first 3 elements, the FIRE would feel comfortable. I'd like to mention it here that there is a video exercise with the 4 elements meditation on my website ex-files.org that would teach you the basic healing and cleansing ways to keep yourself safe.

Next to the years passed, the other era earthlings obsessed with is the future. However, it usually brings you to shiver for different reasons. The beginning of the future is always unclear, so is the end. This uncertainty causes a lot of difficulties where the time still to come is concerned. The flood of questions would keep you back from entering into the territory. What if I made the wrong decision? What if I didn't succeed? What if I did succeed? What if I lived, what if I died? Suddenly every plan, wish or desire collapses and builds a wall between the now and then. The mind is switched to pause, while time passes and life goes on. In the meantime the present is forgotten.

There is a common mistake earthlings do when something interesting or exciting is promised by the future. They dream about it. They want to jump over time to be there as soon as possible, you know, like skipping steps, without realizing that the present – considered to be the real-time life - is passing them by and they miss out on experiences, chances and learning possibilities while eagerly pulling the future nearer. Wishing for the future is just as bad as living in the past. Although time is constantly slowing, it cannot be stopped.

In life, everybody and everything is a mirror that needs to be used for evaluation purposes.

As my experience shows, harmony or balance is widely misunderstood amongst earthlings. Out of the few goals we aim for, this is the most common. We never stop dreaming about it however, deeds usually stay in the background or starts an unrelated journey. We have been fed with fairy tales which show the struggle we need to go through to reach the "*and lived happily ever after*" state and it is always the consequence of marriage, if I put it loosely, a couplehood, between 2 different gendered healthy earthlings, with some sort of wealth behind them to support the harmony they are after. This is a symbolic view of earthly living and should not be taken word for word. The "*what is important is hidden*" theory is in action here once again. Please, read **The Little Prince** by Saint-Exupery! The wedding of the 2 poles means that the interrelations are learned, emotions understood and mastered, and the 2 cosms are united in 1. With the 4 elements existing in harmony, the earthling is ready for the evolution and the quantum leap. This is the marriage we are after; in reality, however, the meaning is concealed behind dogmas, spiritual and religious views that mirror the actual evolutionary level of their creator.

The "*live happily ever after*" concept depicts imaginary state earthlings search for. "*I only want to be happy! Is it too much to ask for?*" we say while waiting for some kind of a miracle, to provide us with the subject or object of our happiness. We do not realize that the question itself is the only obstacle preventing us from reaching a state of harmony. Primarily the sentence is pointed to the Self, and quite rightly I must admit, for happiness comes from within, whatever our understanding of the word is. Nevertheless, we mislead ourselves by pretending to be aware of this. However, on the picture behind this question, there is always somebody taking up a very prominent place in the outcome. Why do we say that "*I want to be happy*" when it is conditioned on the presence of another person? There are 2 answers to this question: we either do not care or we do not understand. Neither of these conditions takes us closer to the goal, due to the lack of a basic understanding of earthly living. Do not expect life to provide you with goodies, only because you feel superior and above it. Start a conversation, establish the goal and make a move. Otherwise, life doesn't know what you are after. Remember, it is a love-affair.

Earthlings are here to evolve through experience. Basically, there are two kinds of experiences: conscious and random. Although they both further the journey, in this case, I talk about spiritual experience and not of money-making skills, as I pointed out earlier. Earthlings who are aware of the path set their goals with an understanding that they are only necessary for drawing the initial direction, rather than an aim to reach. Random experiences are thrown in by the Universe to help the evolutionary journey. As everything is interrelated, these events are actually the consequences of the energy movements in one's life. Earthlings who are spiritually aware would be grateful for and learn from both. Others would get angry, depressed, hurt and unhappy about the random experiences, and would hurry to reach the goal they consciously set without walking the path towards it.

It does not matter which way I look at the interrelation of energies in human relationships, the Self has to be built in order to understand that you are responsible for not only your deeds, words, and thoughts but for those of every human being because you are also affected by their deeds, words, and thoughts.

It is very easy to get lost on the road to fulfilment. However, one thing is for sure: there is no easy way, and spiritual development is a must. The fear of being different keeps a lot of people away from this search and the misconception concerning the meaning of spirituality and religion only adds to the task load.

Just to remind you, I put it in front of you again.

Religion is a set of beliefs and practices often centred upon specific supernatural and moral claims about reality. Becoming part of a religious group only requires acceptance of the mentioned beliefs; while spirituality is an individual and sometimes lonely path to walk, in order to become one with the Creator Force and gain the highest level of existence open to earthlings.

Looking at our world at the moment there are different groups, trying to push, sometimes even force earthlings into an agreement of their theories in life, by limiting their views of the Universe and promising salvation for deeds they consider improper for a human being. Needless to say, the choice is yours. Occasionally one might be forced into joining certain assemblies nevertheless, the real and the only freedom dwells in the mind, regardless of the behaviour pattern of the physical body. Only the freedom of thoughts is not limited by societies and powers. Do not let them win.

Religious groups and individuals who denounce the exchange of energies between earthlings in any way, are hiding away from the pleasure, sorrow, happiness, sadness and the other feelings encountered through this type of exchange. As practice shows, their auras are pale and the fire is missing from them, together with the element of Earth. One might say that being connected to the Creator Force is all one needs and that knowledge finds a way to flow into the consciousness of the individual. However, we are here to learn and go through certain events and to understand the Creator – meaning the first knowledge that was able to multiply by division – within. Without this wisdom, one cannot get connected to it, through the dividend created between the two worlds.

Now that we have the disastrous Covid-19 amongst us, certain religious leaders and many followers would condemn earthling of different beliefs as the cause of the pandemic. But why does it enter anyone's mind that God or whatever you want to call it, favours one group over the other? Why do people want to side with such a creator force, who wants worshipping and favours and whatever else the leaders decide, to keep them in his/her heart? The whole universe and everything in it is his/her creation! Why would he/she neglect one over the other? Isn't it a really deceitful naturalistic? I think human beings create their Gods to mirror their limited understanding and behaviour pattern.

Here, I would like to give you a story of a student of mine, who also is a good friend as all my students. She is having physical coordination problems that nobody can diagnose. We have been working on it together. One day, I sent her to a certain place during Alchemy lesson and she came back with the following:

"Back in time, I had a situation where I chose to care about my emotions instead of standing up for myself. I need to learn to set boundaries and it will

make me strong again. Nobody will find a reason why my body is deteriorating because it comes from within so stop wasting time and money going to doctors. The only way to eat the fish is to kill it and cut the head of. If I feel sorry for the fish instead of caring about myself, I will stay hungry."

Life is a delicate catch 22. In the cycle, organic energies co-exist by understanding that they are all important, all have purpose and chores to perform, and feed on each other.

Although not the most intelligent but the most complex of them all is humanity. It is due to the fact that earthlings are not born into the cycle of nature on the planet. They need to lift themselves up by raising emotional intelligence and awareness, to actually fit the requirements. Perhaps, it is the reason why those surviving on slow energies, don't care about this cycle, for they lack the understanding and cannot see its importance. The comprehension of the whole scenario is limited. When a human being runs out of control, we usually compare his actions to those of certain animals by saying, that he is a beast and he behaves like an animal. If you think about it, only human beings are capable of killing missions, cruelties, mental and emotional tortures. That is why conscious learning is vital.

I have mentioned the micro and the macrocosm a few times in this book. It is time to add some clarification. Everybody's micro and macrocosm are different. The microcosm is the comfort zone that could be the bedroom or the universe. It is the place one understands – or thinks safe - and the rest will be the macrocosm. During our existence we expand the microcosm by learning and experiencing.

The lives of earthlings are filled with illusions. These are imaginary good and bad to ease their fear. Security is one of them. It doesn't exist. The only secure point in their lives is trust in the self. Everything else is in constant motion, therefore changing.

Life is full of choices! Make the choice and pursue it. However, call upon your intelligence when you are at it. Here is my motto:

"God, give me the Serenity

To accept the thing I cannot change,

Courage to change the things I can,

And Wisdom always to see the Difference."

I wish you a good life!

AKIA Philosophy®

AKIA carries the total understanding of the interrelation between the micro - and macrocosm, looks upon everything as an essential part of the whole and upon the whole as an essential part of everything, for all organic and inorganic energies enjoys the same level of importance. This belief makes up the strong foundation of AKIA philosophy.

AKIA is the philosophy of the unseen soul and cosmic knowledge. The philosophy that sets you free.

According to **AKIA Philosophy®** everything and everybody is energy. Energy in the sense of physics. These energies are either organic - meaning living - or non-organic - meaning not capable of multiplying or any other form of reproduction. These energies have every feature of the energy known from physics. They have speed, frequency, sound, smell, taste, consistency, colour and polarity. Very obviously these energies are interrelated. This interrelation is the motion of life.

The spirituality of mankind started to vanish when the word 'individuality' appeared in our life. By ignoring the interrelation of energies we were faced with a mass of new and frustratingly unsolvable questions that made our lives very insecure and doubtful. The mad search for understanding and knowing was launched. According to AKIA one cannot and need not understand everything. That is the profound understanding of this philosophy.

Through the milestones, AKIA proves, that one is the whole and the whole is the one, meaning that everything leads back to one source, the God source, the Creator. The Creator - let it be a stone, a cloud or a tree - is the first knowledge that was able to multiply by division. Following this sense, a soul is a knowledge that is able to multiply by division.

AKIA says that one can only understand oneself through the Universe. Also says that everything is always in motion and constantly changing. This interrelation of energies warns us that we are responsible not only for ourselves, but everybody and everything for everybody and everything affect us, our state of mind, our way of thinking, health and behaviour pattern.

AKIA has been created and founded by Zsa Zsa Tudos philosopher, teacher, healer, international clairvoyant and author.

AKIA Philosophy® is the registered trademark of our teachings.

https://ex-files.org

https://akialight.com

https://akiaphilosophy.com

Akia-Path-Finder

1.   Time is an illusion that imprisons those without courage

2. Life is a constant cycle of personal truth searching

3. Live without bringing shame on yourself

4. You must remake yourself in the eternity of your body

5. The night is not the end of a bad day but the beginning of a better one

6. The outside knowledge is the start of the wisdom within

7. Wisdom is the knowledge you can make use of

8. Material wealth you can inherit, however, true dignity you need to work for

9. Everything you can touch is lent to you for this life. When you leave you cannot take them with you

10. Only through the Universe you can get to know yourself

11. The light embraces you unconditionally and disappears in you if you let it

12. Imagination is the memory of the soul

13. The real knowledge is untouchable and changing

Other books from the author:

- **5 Secrets of The Matrix –** True Core of Self-Development
- **Emotion the Machinery of Life** – The Missing Factors of Happy Relationships
- **Heavenly nourishment** – Conscious eating in 7 steps
- **Intersextion** – and they work together
- **The 4th Way** – Teaching the Gnostic Wisdom of AKIA Philosophy
- **Pandemic** – The story of mankind
- **Dancing with the Desertwolf –** Life my Eternal Love
- **The Five Minutes Man and the Girl who Fell in Love with Mint**

THANK YOU FOR LEAVING A REVIEW!

We are devoted to help find the Self and the Path towards fulfilment.

Check out our free introductory webinars on

Regain your Wisdom/Mindblower Masterclass.

Reserve your seat here

https://akiaphilosophy.com/regain-your-wisdom/

Subscribe to newsletter here:

https://ex-files.org/newsletter/